VAN HALEN BEST OF

VOLUME I

C O N T E N T S

Project Manager: Aaron Stang
Music Editor: Colgan Bryan
CD Art Direction: Stine Schyberg
Photography: Michael LLewellyn
Book Art Layout: Ken Rehm

DANCE THE NIGHT AWAY

Words and Music by
EDWARD VAN HALEN, ALEX VAN HALEN,
MICHAEL ANTHONY and DAVID LEE ROTH

4

Dance the Night Away - 9 - 4
PG9665

8

Dance the Night Away - 9 - 6
PG9665

*First note of Riff B is tied, not struck (all times).

Dance the Night Away - 9 - 9
PG9665

ERUPTION

Words and Music by
EDWARD VAN HALEN, ALEX VAN HALEN,
MICHAEL ANTHONY and DAVID LEE ROTH

Tune down 1/2 step:
⑥ = Eb ③ = Gb
⑤ = Ab ② = Bb
④ = Db ① = Eb

*w/slight flanging and tape echo delay.

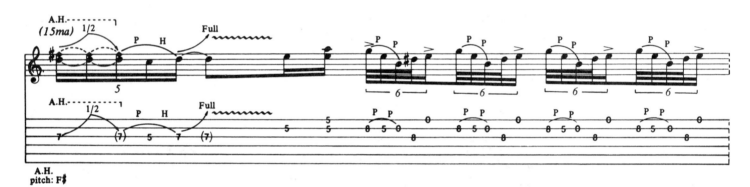

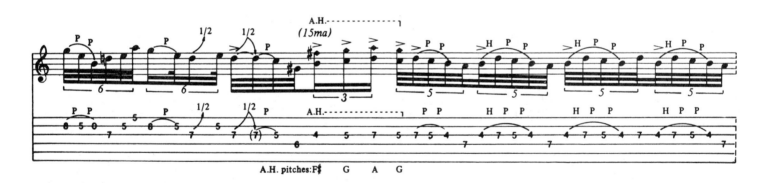

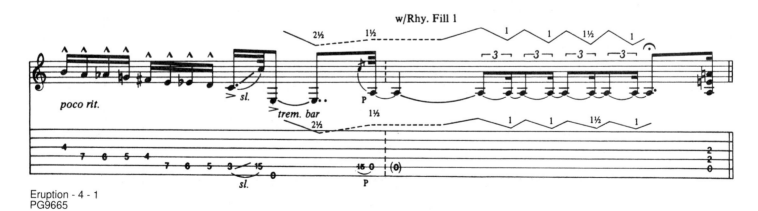

Eruption - 4 - 1
PG9665

*Release finger pressure when arriving at 19fr. at end of slide to sound F♯ natural harmonic.

Rhy. Fill 1

Overdubbed gtr.

Eruption - 4 - 2
PG9665

14

*w/more intense flanging.

*w/flanger (slow sweep, medium intensity & regeneration)
& tape echo delay (approx. 150 ms. w/one repeat).

*Slightly rushed.

Eruption - 4 - 3
PG9665

AIN'T TALKIN' 'BOUT LOVE

Words and Music by
EDWARD VAN HALEN, ALEX VAN HALEN,
MICHAEL ANTHONY and DAVID LEE ROTH

*Echo at approx. 100 ms. delay, flanger w/slow speed,
w/regeneration sweep & moderate depth.

**A.H. pitch alternates between 8va & 15ma as a result of flange sweep.

Ain't Talkin' 'Bout Love - 8 - 1
PG9665

*Fret chord with trem. bar partially depressed, strike chord, quickly return bar to pitch and slide chord shape down in fast gliss.

RUNNIN' WITH THE DEVIL

Words and Music by
EDWARD VAN HALEN, ALEX VAN HALEN,
MICHAEL ANTHONY and DAVID LEE ROTH

Runnin' with the Devil - 6 - 1
PG9665

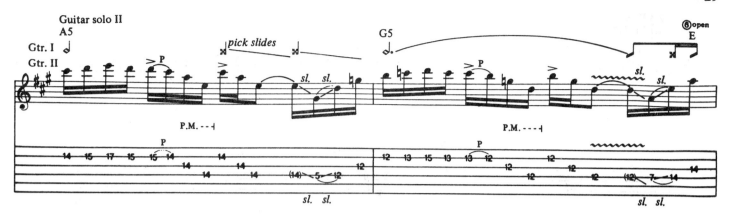

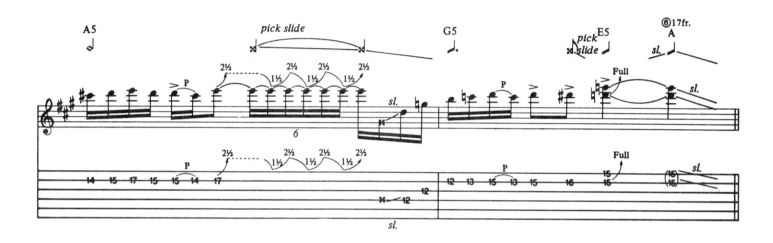

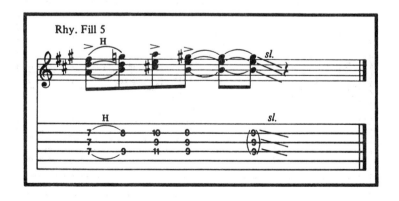

AND THE CRADLE WILL ROCK

Words and Music by
EDWARD VAN HALEN, ALEX VAN HALEN,
MICHAEL ANTHONY and DAVID LEE ROTH

And the Cradle Will Rock - 8 - 1
PG9665

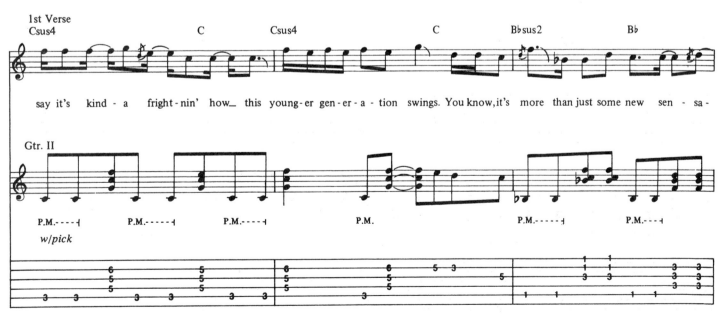

And the Cradle Will Rock - 8 - 3
PG9665

Yes, the cra-dle, cra-dle will rock.__ And I say, rock on!

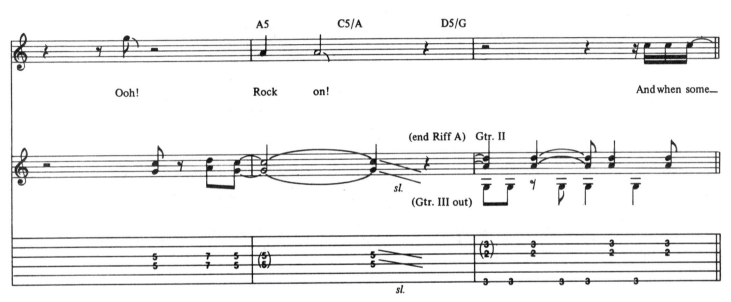

Ooh! Rock on! And when some__

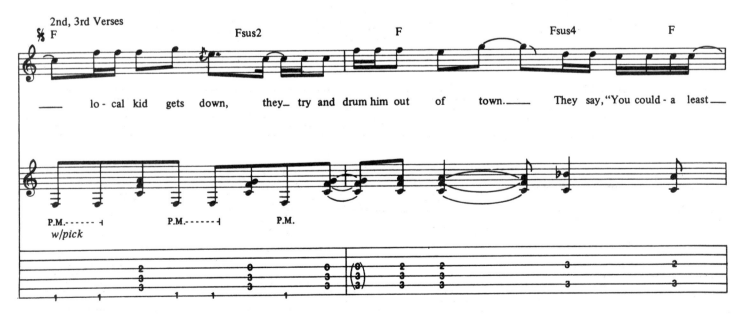

__ lo-cal kid gets down, they__ try and drum him out of town.__ They say, "You could-a least__

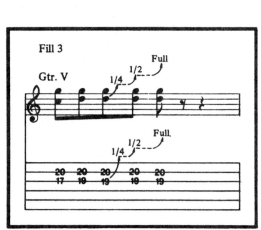

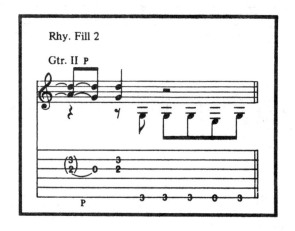

And the Cradle Will Rock - 8 - 8
PG9665

UNCHAINED

Words and Music by
EDWARD VAN HALEN, ALEX VAN HALEN,
MICHAEL ANTHONY and DAVID LEE ROTH

Unchained - 12 - 1
PG9665

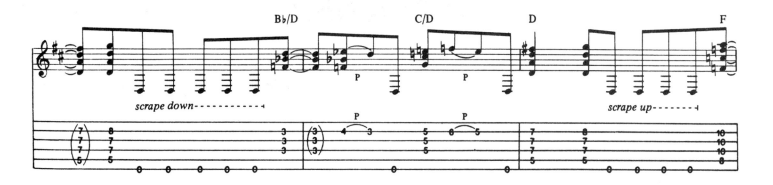

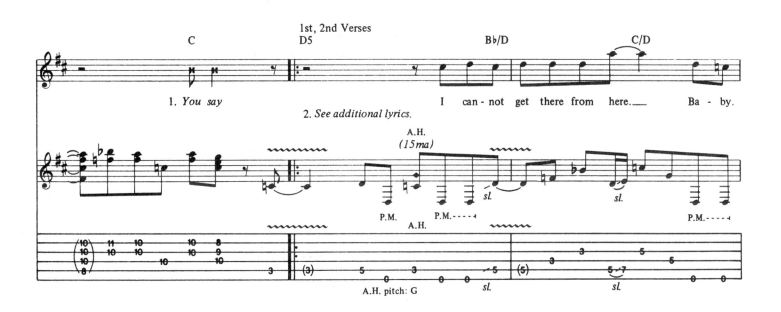

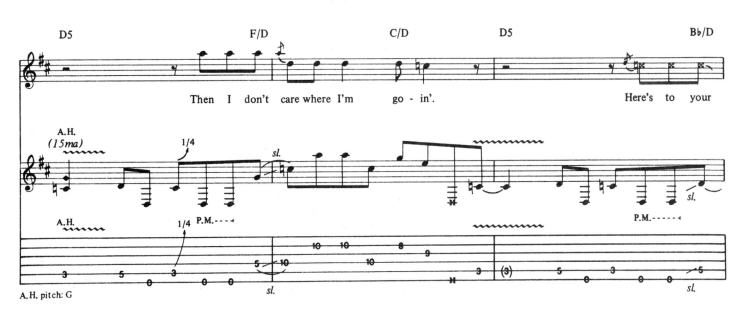

40

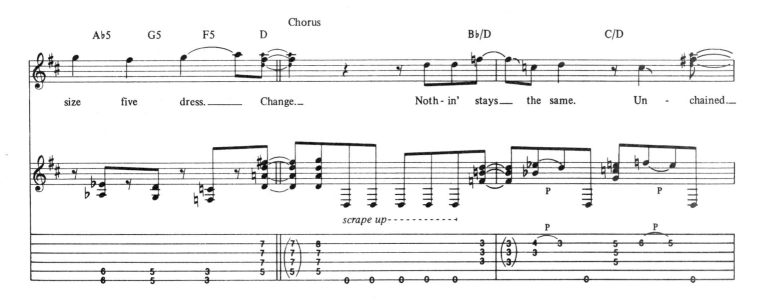

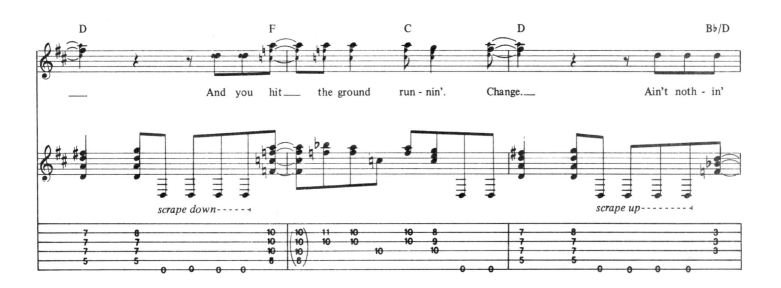

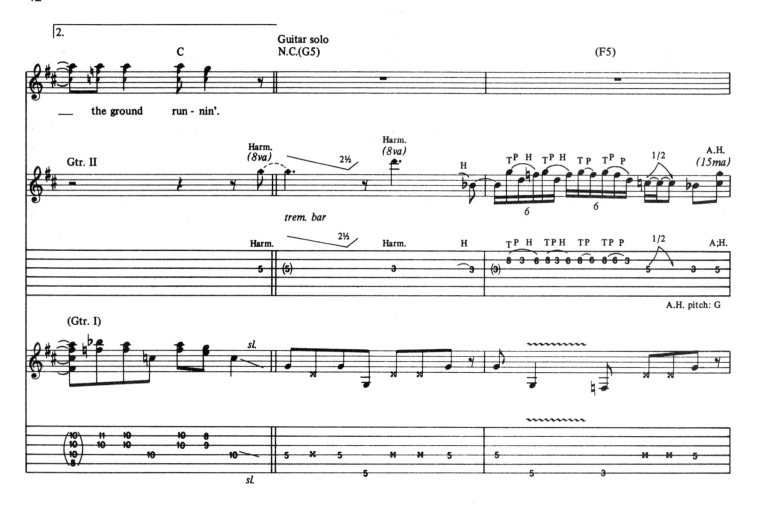

the ground   run - nin'.

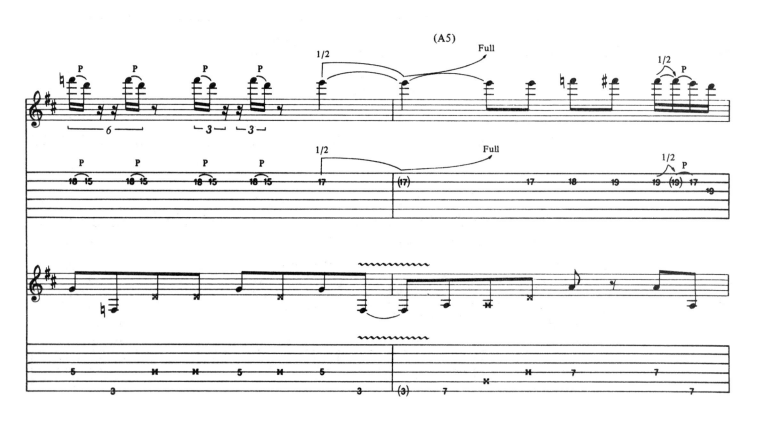

44

stays the same. Un - chained___ Yeah, you hit___ the ground run - nin'.

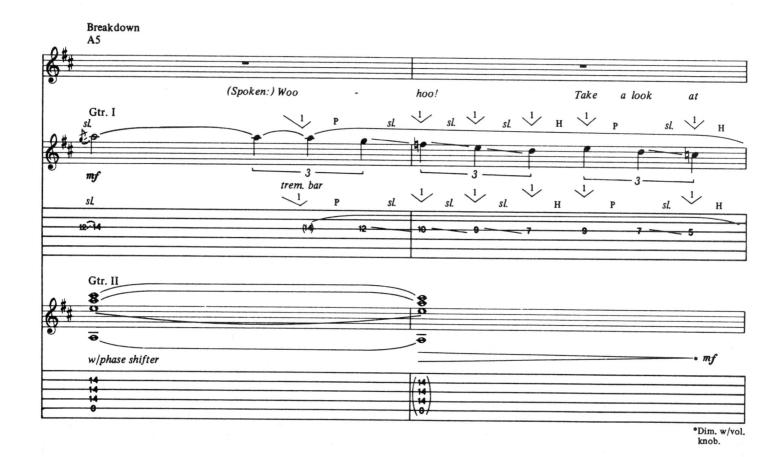

(Spoken:) Woo - hoo! Take a look at

*Dim. w/vol.
knob.

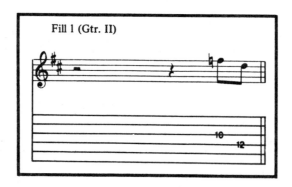

Fill 1 (Gtr. II)

G/A   D/A   A5(7)

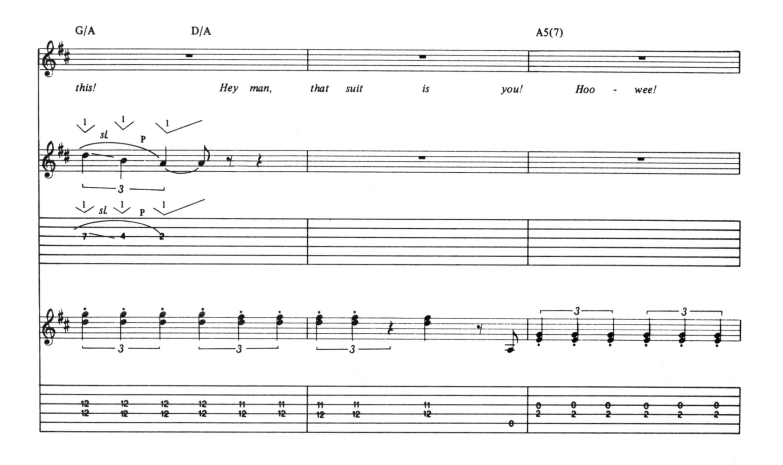

this!   Hey man,   that   suit   is   you!   Hoo - wee!

A5   A5(7)

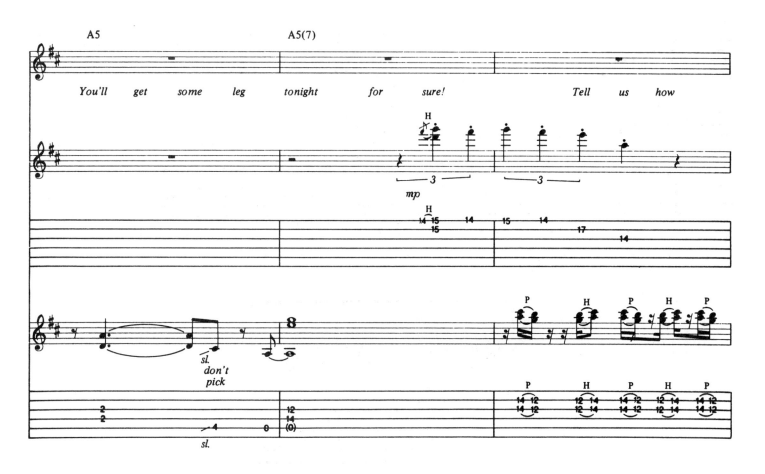

You'll   get   some   leg   tonight   for   sure!   Tell   us   how

*Tapped harmonic.

*Pick slide.

48

Unchained - 12 - 11
PG9665

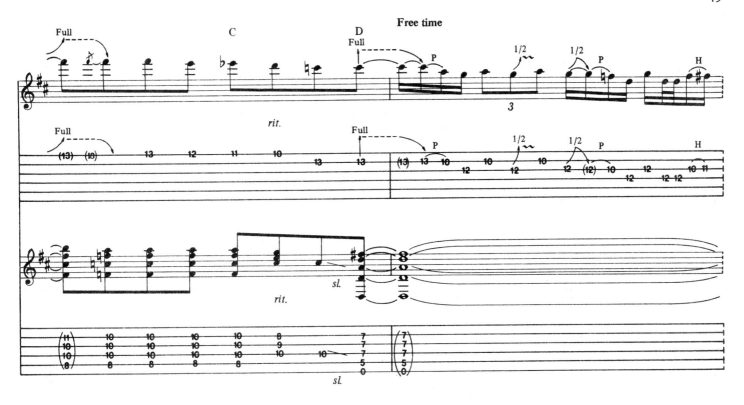

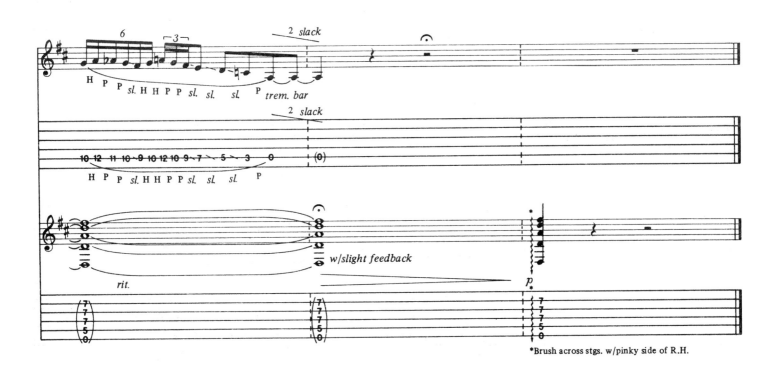

*Brush across stgs. w/pinky side of R.H.

Additional Lyrics

2. I know I don't ask for permission.
This is my chance to fly.
Maybe enough ain't enough for you,
But it's my turn to try. *(To Pre-chorus)*

JUMP

Words and Music by
EDWARD VAN HALEN, ALEX VAN HALEN,
MICHAEL ANTHONY and DAVID LEE ROTH

Jump - 6 - 1
PG9665

*Chord names derived from bass and synth. (next 8 bars).
**Tune down 1/2 step. Music sounds as written.

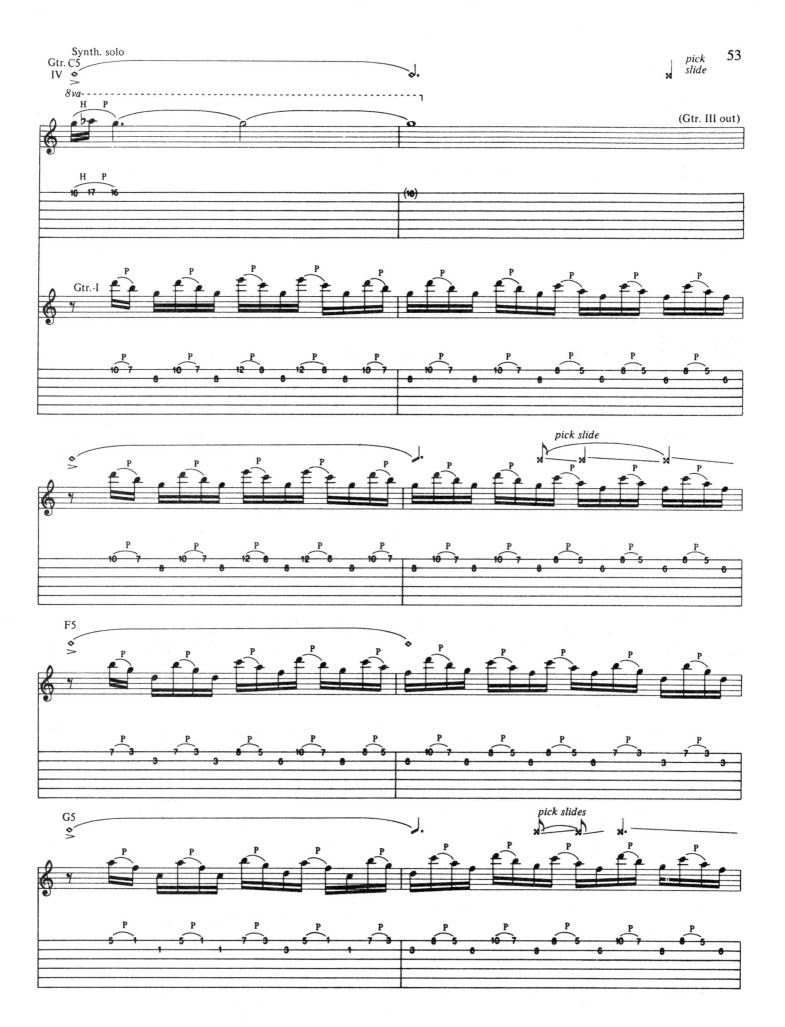

54

*T =Tap w/R.H. index finger.
(T)=Tap w/R.H. ring finger.
(P)=Pull-off to R.H. index finger.

w/Riff A

Out-chorus
w/Riff A (3 times)

jump. (Jump!)   Go a-head and   jump._   Get in and

Gtr. II

PANAMA

Words and Music by
EDWARD VAN HALEN, ALEX VAN HALEN,
MICHAEL ANTHONY and DAVID LEE ROTH

Panama - 8 - 1
PG9665

Panama - 8 - 2
PG9665

58

2nd Verse

62

Panama - 8 - 7
PG9665

WHY CAN'T THIS BE LOVE

Words and Music by
EDWARD VAN HALEN, ALEX VAN HALEN,
MICHAEL ANTHONY and SAMMY HAGAR

Whoa,_____ here it comes,____ that fun-ny feel-ing a-gain,___ wind-ing me

Why Can't This Be Love - 8 - 2
PG9665

66

Bridge

N.C.

Da doo da doo da doo da da da doo da doo da doo da_ da doo da da doo da doo da doo da da doo da doo da doo da_

Guitar solo

N.C.

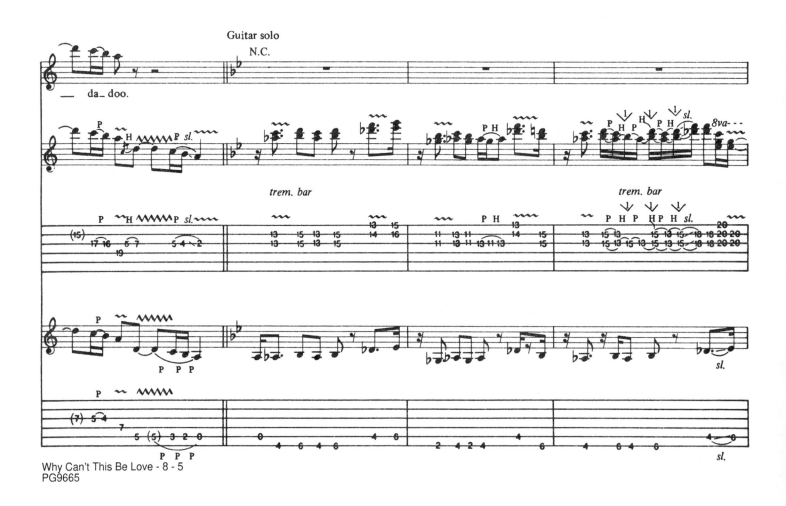

_ da_ doo.

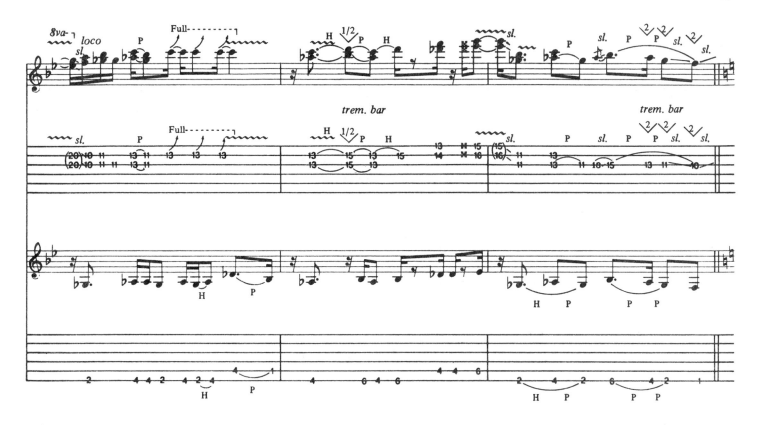

Da doo da doo da doo da da da doo da doo da doo da da da doo da da doo da da doo da doo da da doo da doo da da doo da doo da doo da da doo da doo da doo da

70

000000000

00000

Ba-by, why can't this be love? Got to know why can't this be love?

I wan-na know why can't this be love?

Begin fade

N.C.

Gtr. II

Fade out

Gtr. I

Why Can't This Be Love - 8 - 8
PG9665

DREAMS

Words and Music by
EDWARD VAN HALEN, SAMMY HAGAR,
MICHAEL ANTHONY and ALEX VAN HALEN

Dreams - 10 - 1
PG9665

the cracks._____ Stand-in' on bro-ken dreams,___ nev-er los-

ing_ sight._ Ah!_ Well, just spread your_ wings._____ We'll get

So ba-by, dry_____ your_ eyes, _

_ save _____ all _____ the tears_____ you've_

cried. Oh, _____ that's what dreams_

78

Dreams - 10 - 7
PG9665

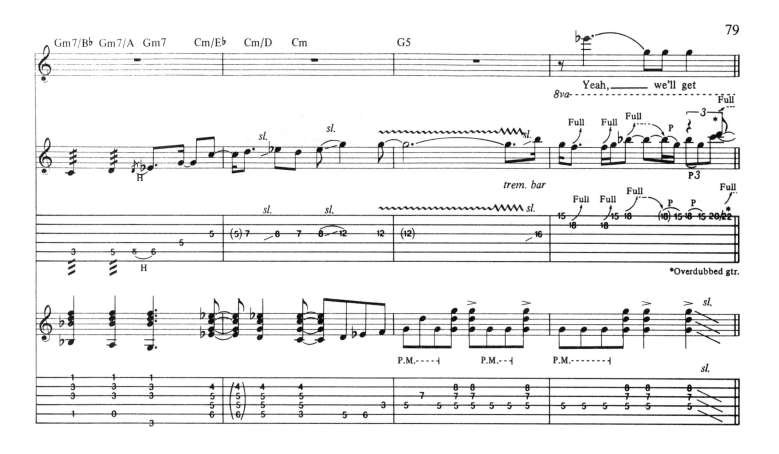

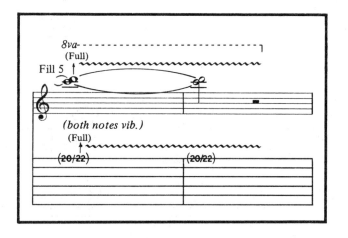

RIGHT NOW

Words and Music by
EDWARD VAN HALEN, ALEX VAN HALEN,
MICHAEL ANTHONY and SAMMY HAGAR

84

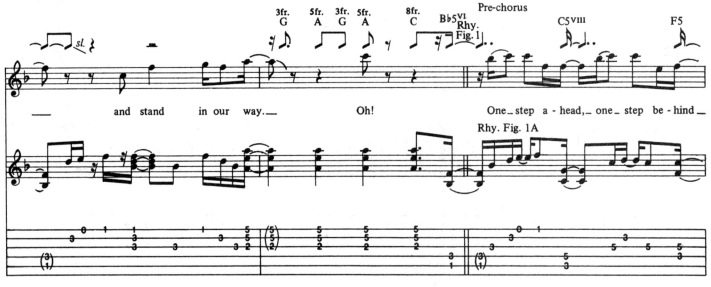

86

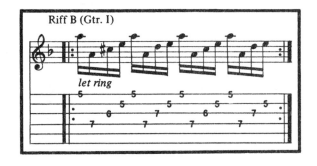

88

Additional Lyrics

2. Miss a beat, you lose the rhythm
   And nothing falls into place.
   Only missed by a fraction,
   Sent a little off your pace.

2nd Pre-chorus:
   The more things you get, the more you want.
   Just tradin' one for the other.
   Workin' so hard to make it easy.
   Got to turn, come on, turn this thing around. *(To Chorus)*

Right Now - 7 - 7
PG9665

VAN HALEN

1 RUNNIN' WITH THE DEVIL 2 ERUPTION 3 YOU REALLY GOT ME 4 AIN'T
TALKIN' 'BOUT LOVE 5 I'M THE ONE 6 JAMIE'S CRYIN' 7 ATOMIC PUNK
8 FEEL YOUR LOVE TONIGHT 9 LITTLE DREAMER 10 ICE
CREAM MAN 11 ON FIRE

PRODUCED BY TED TEMPLEMAN

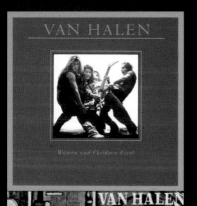

VAN HALEN II

1979

1 YOU'RE NO GOOD 2 DANCE THE NIGHT AWAY
3 SOMEBODY GET ME A DOCTOR 4 BOTTOMS
UP! 5 OUTTA LOVE AGAIN 6 LIGHT UP THE SKY
7 SPANISH FLY 8 D.O.A. 9 WOMEN IN LOVE...
10 BEAUTIFUL GIRLS

PRODUCED BY TED TEMPLEMAN

WOMEN AND CHILDREN FIRST

1980

1 AND THE CRADLE WILL ROCK... 2 EVERYBODY
WANTS SOME!! 3 FOOLS 4 ROMEO DELIGHT
5 TORA! TORA! 6 LOSS OF CONTROL 7 TAKE THE
WHISKEY HOME 8 COULD THIS BE MAGIC? 9 IN A
SIMPLE RHYME

PRODUCED BY TED TEMPLEMAN

FAIR WARNING

1981

1 MEAN STREET 2 "DIRTY MOVIES" 3 SINNER'S SWING! 4 HEAR ABOUT IT
LATER 5 UNCHAINED
6 PUSH COMES TO SHOVE 7 SO THIS IS LOVE?
8 SUNDAY AFTERNOON IN THE PARK 9 ONE
FOOT OUT THE DOOR

PRODUCED BY TED TEMPLEMAN

DIVER DOWN

1982

1 WHERE HAVE ALL THE GOOD TIMES GONE! 2 HANG 'EM HIGH 3
CATHEDRAL 4 SECRETS 5 INTRUDER 6 (OH) PRETTY WOMAN 7
DANCING IN THE STREET
8 LITTLE GUITARS (INTRO) 9 LITTLE GUITARS 10 BIG BAD
BILL (IS SWEET WILLIAM NOW) 11 THE FULL
BUG 12 HAPPY TRAILS

PRODUCED BY TED TEMPLEMAN

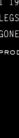

1984

1984

1 1984 2 JUMP 3 PANAMA 4 TOP JIMMY 5 DROP DEAD
LEGS 6 HOT FOR TEACHER 7 I'LL WAIT 8 GIRL
GONE BAD 9 HOUSE OF PAIN

PRODUCED BY TED TEMPLEMAN

5150 · 1986

1 GOOD ENOUGH 2 WHY CAN'T THIS BE LOVE 3 GET UP 4
DREAMS 5 SUMMER NIGHTS 6 BEST OF BOTH WORLDS
7 LOVE WALKS IN 8 "5150" 9 INSIDE
PRODUCED BY VAN HALEN, MICK JONES
AND DONN LANDEE

OU812 · 1988

1 MINE ALL MINE 2 WHEN IT'S LOVE 3 A.F.U.
(NATURALLY WIRED) 4 CABO WABO 5 SOURCE OF INFECTION
6 FEELS SO GOOD 7 FINISH WHAT YA STARTED 8 BLACK AND
BLUE 9 SUCKER IN A
3 PIECE 10 A APOLITICAL BLUES
RECORDED BY DONN LANDEE

FOR UNLAWFUL CARNAL KNOWLEDGE · 1991

1 POUNDCAKE 2 JUDGEMENT DAY 3 SPANKED
4 RUNAROUND 5 PLEASURE DOME 6 IN 'N' OUT 7 MAN
ON A MISSION 8 THE DREAM IS OVER 9 RIGHT NOW
10 316 11 TOP OF THE WORLD
PRODUCED BY ANDY JOHNS, TED TEMPLEMAN
AND VAN HALEN

LIVE: RIGHT HERE, RIGHT NOW · 1993

DISC ONE 1 POUNDCAKE 2 JUDGEMENT DAY 3 WHEN IT'S
LOVE 4 SPANKED 5 AIN'T TALKIN' 'BOUT LOVE 6 IN
'N' OUT 7 DREAMS 8 MAN ON A MISSION 9 ULTRA BASS
10 PLEASURE DOME/DRUM SOLO 11 PANAMA 12 LOVE
WALKS IN 13 RUNAROUND DISC TWO 1 RIGHT NOW 2 ONE
WAY TO ROCK 3 WHY CAN'T THIS BE LOVE 4 GIVE TO
LIVE 5 FINISH WHAT YA STARTED 6 BEST OF BOTH
WORLDS 7 316 8 YOU REALLY GOT ME/CABO WABO
9 WON'T GET FOOLED AGAIN 10 JUMP 11 TOP OF THE
WORLD
PRODUCED BY VAN HALEN AND ANDY JOHNS

BALANCE · 1995

1 THE SEVENTH SEAL 2 CAN'T STOP LOVIN' YOU
3 DON'T TELL ME (WHAT LOVE CAN DO) 4 AMSTER-
DAM 5 BIG FAT MONEY 6 AFTERSHOCK 7 STRUNG OUT
8 NOT ENOUGH 9 DOIN' TIME 10 BALUCHITHERIUM
11 TAKE ME BACK (DEJA VU) 12 FEELIN'
PRODUCED BY BRUCE FAIRBAIRN

POUNDCAKE

Words and Music by
EDWARD VAN HALEN, ALEX VAN HALEN,
MICHAEL ANTHONY and SAMMY HAGAR

98

Poundcake - 13 - 6
PG9665

100

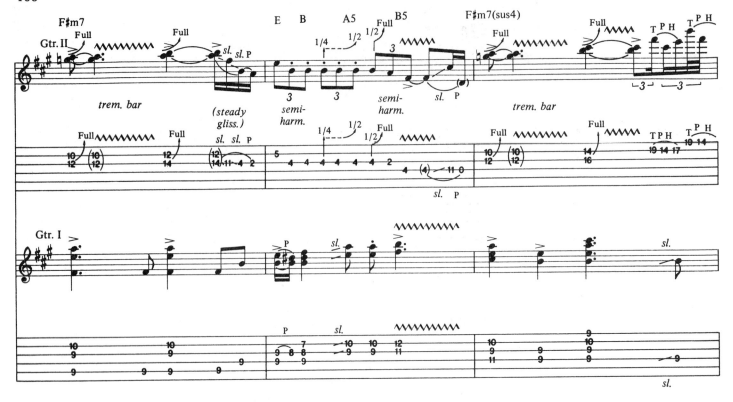

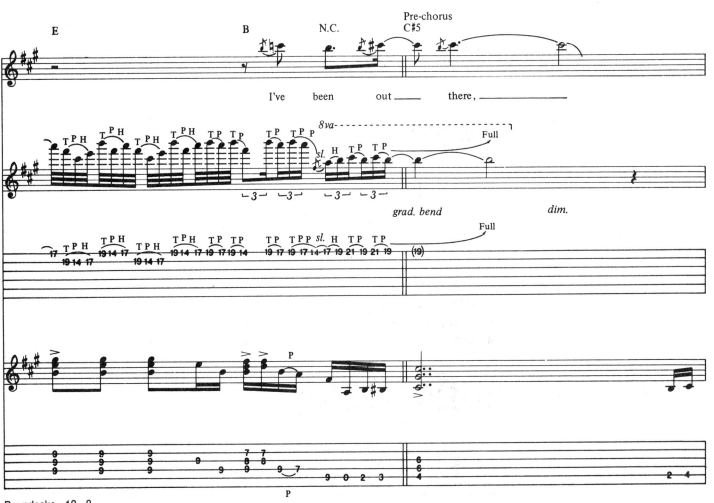

Poundcake - 13 - 8
PG9665

*Two gtrs. One gtr. allows chords to sustain while other plays harmonics.

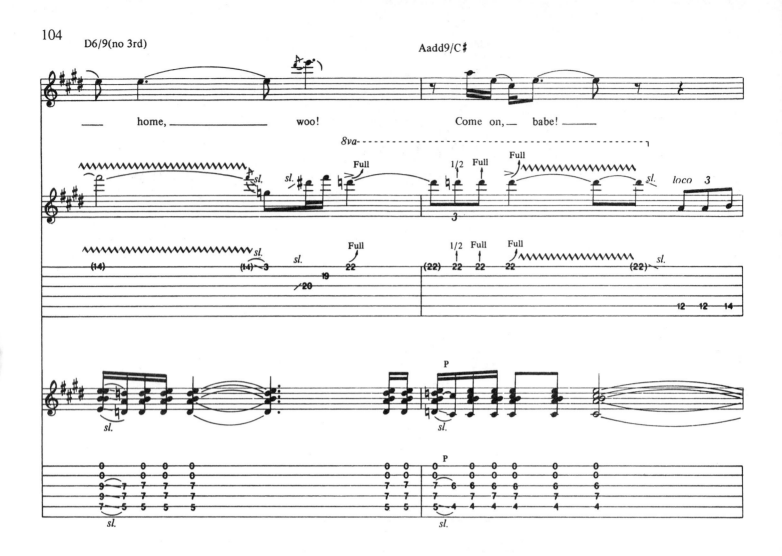

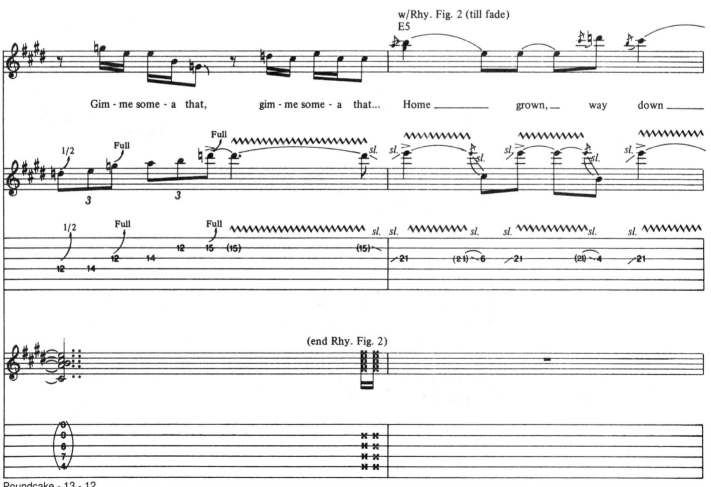

WHEN IT'S LOVE

**Words and Music by
EDWARD VAN HALEN, ALEX VAN HALEN,
MICHAEL ANTHONY and SAMMY HAGAR**

*Combined gtr. & synth. riff (Gtr. I), Gtr. III in upstems. Bass in steady 8ths.

*Synth. chords arr. for gtr.
**Synth. bass arr. for gtr.

When It's Love - 6 - 2
PG9665

108

When It's Love - 6 - 3
PG9665

110

When It's Love - 6 - 5
PG9665

CAN'T STOP LOVIN' YOU

Words and Music by
EDDIE VAN HALEN, ALEX VAN HALEN,
SAMMY HAGAR and MICHAEL ANTHONY

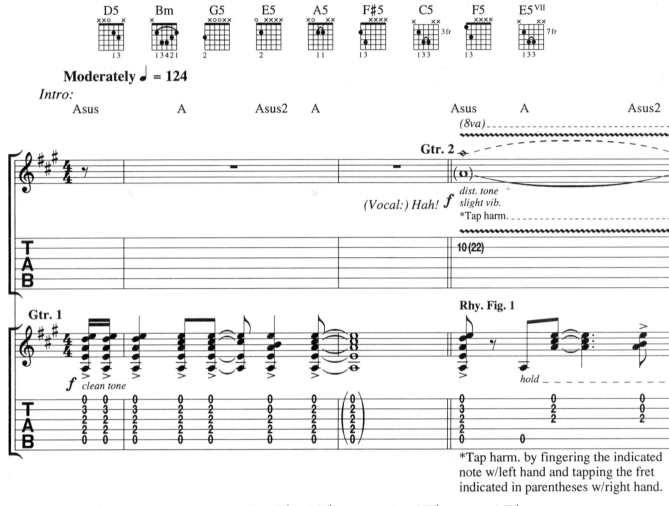

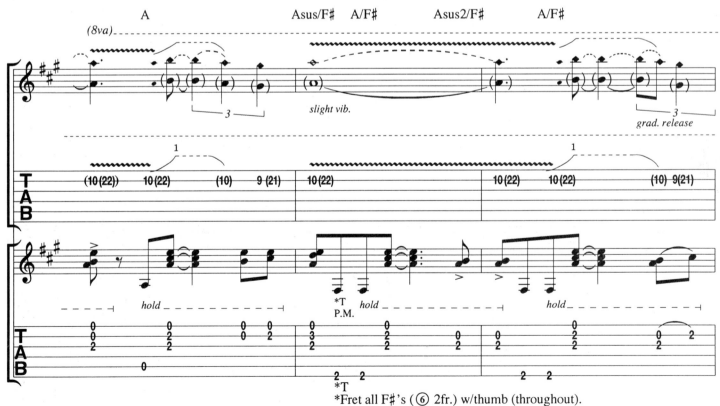

*Fret all F#'s (⑥ 2fr.) w/thumb (throughout).

Can't Stop Lovin' You – 12 – 1
PG9665

114

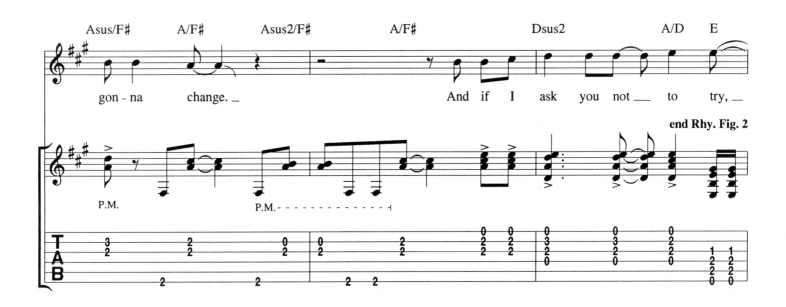

Can't Stop Lovin' You – 12 – 3
PG9665

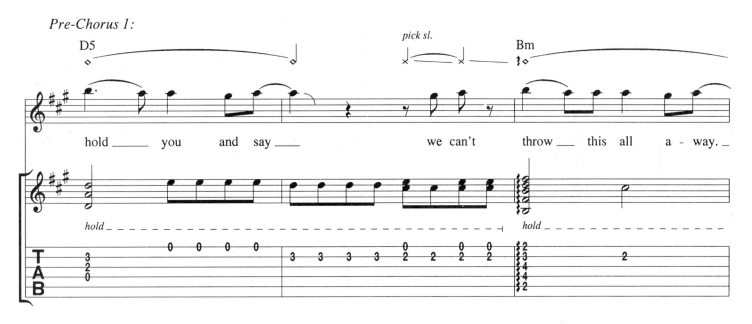

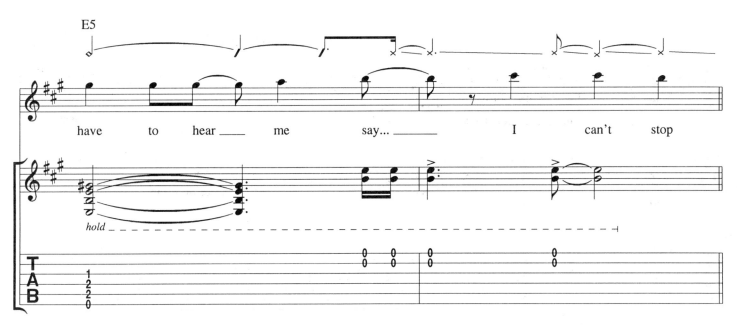

Can't Stop Lovin' You – 12 – 4
PG9665

116

Pre-Chorus 2:

120

*Gradually increase width of vib.

Bridge 2:

w/Bkgd. Voc. Fig. 2

HUMANS BEING

Words and Music by
**EDDIE VAN HALEN, ALEX VAN HALEN,
SAMMY HAGAR and MICHAEL ANTHONY**

*Repeat ad lib. simile throughout.

*During verses, lead vocal is doubled one octave lower
w/slight variations ad lib. (throughout).

Humans Being – 13 – 1
PG9665

al - most guilt - y. Is that why God made us breed, to make us see we're

hu - mans be - ing?

Gtr. 2

Gtr. 1

126

Verses 2 & 3:

w/Rhy. Fig. 1 (Gtr. 1) 1 1/2 times

2. You break this, I'll break all that. You break my back with
   low-life, flat-head scum in-fects. The sick-ness back in his

**Gtr. 2

*Vocal harmony Verse 1 only.
**Gtr. 2 Verse 2 only; Verse 3 tacet.

all   your   crap. Spread your dis-ease like lem-mings breed-ing,
eyes re-flects. You won-der why your life is scream-ing,

*Pre-bend w/trem. bar.

Humans Being – 13 – 3
PG9665

128

*Pre-bend w/trem. bar.

Humans Being – 13 – 5
PG9665

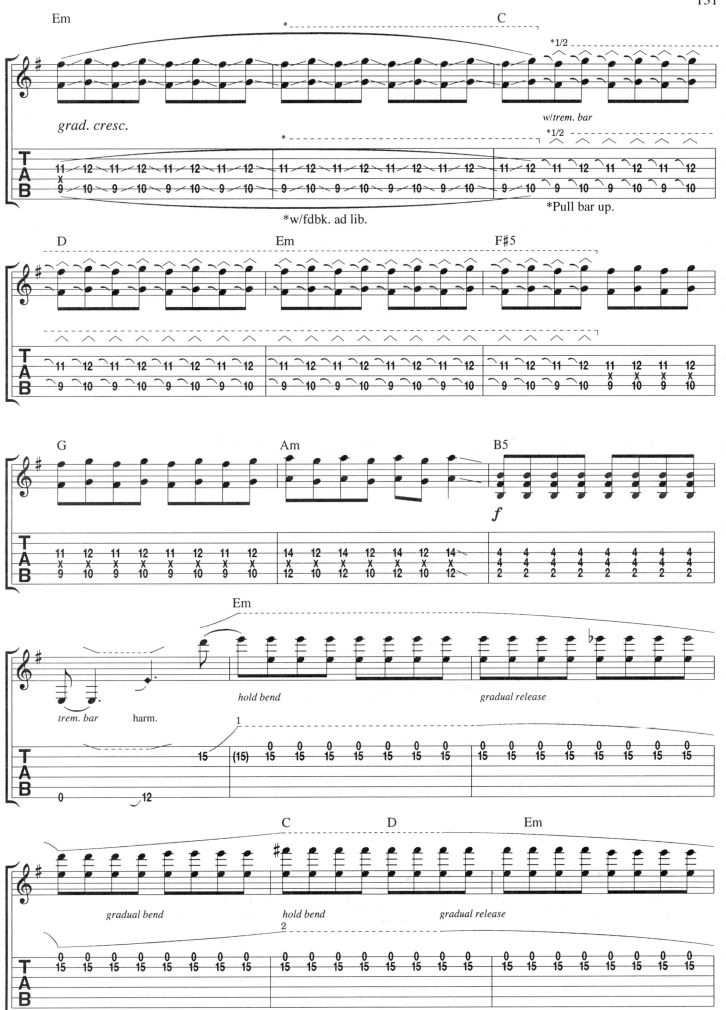

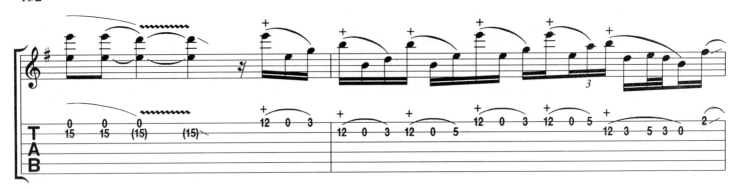

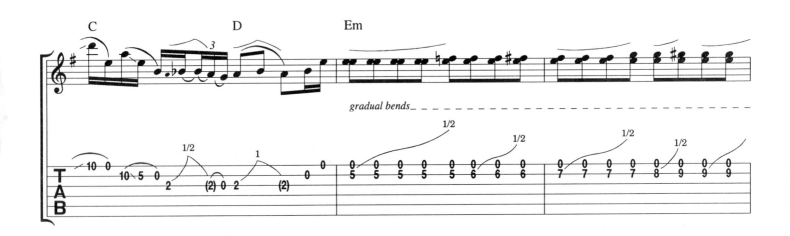

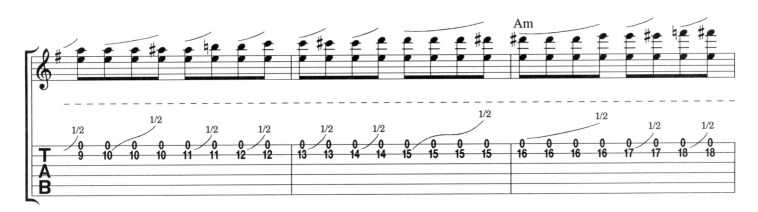

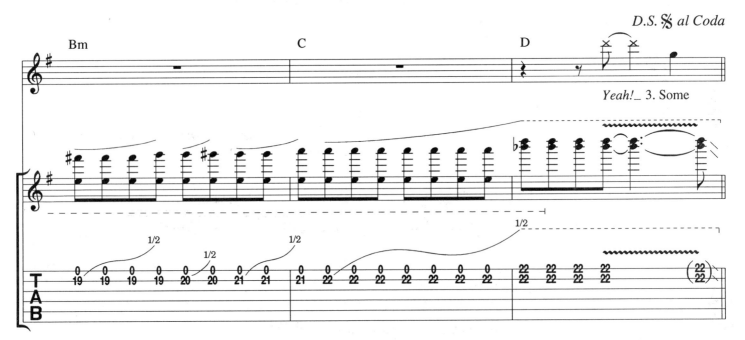

Coda

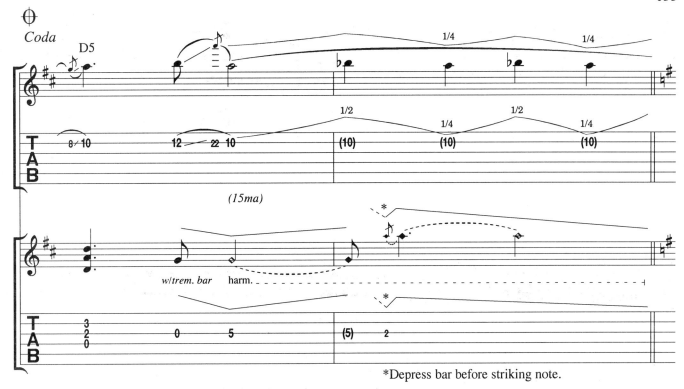

*Depress bar before striking note.

Outro:

w/Rhy. Fig. 1 *(Gtr. 1) till end*

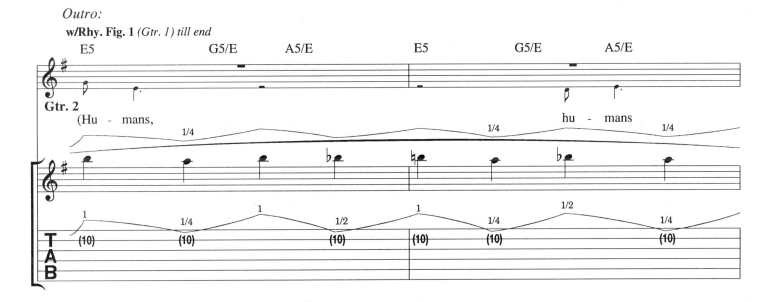

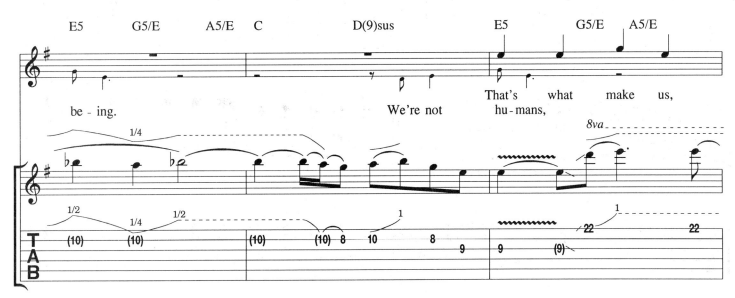

134

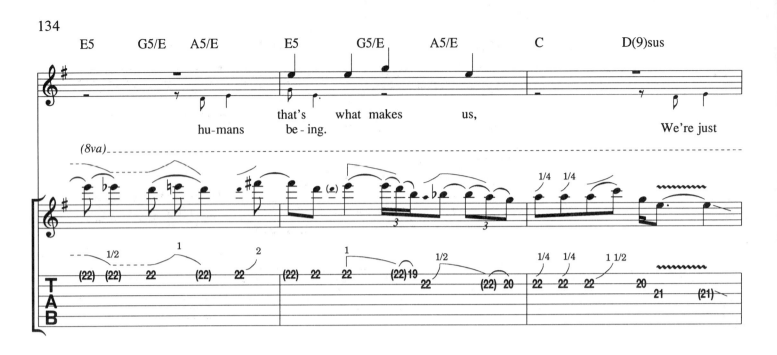

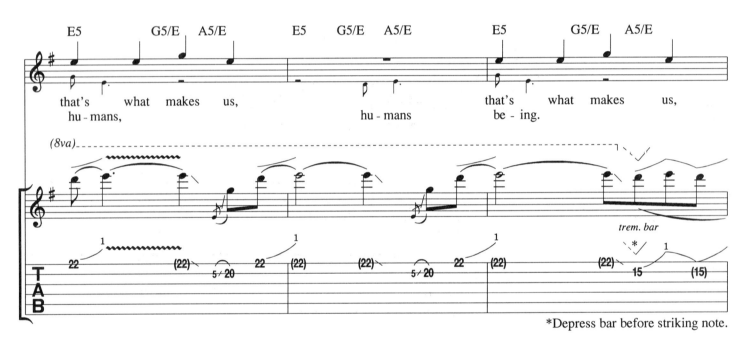

*Depress bar before striking note.

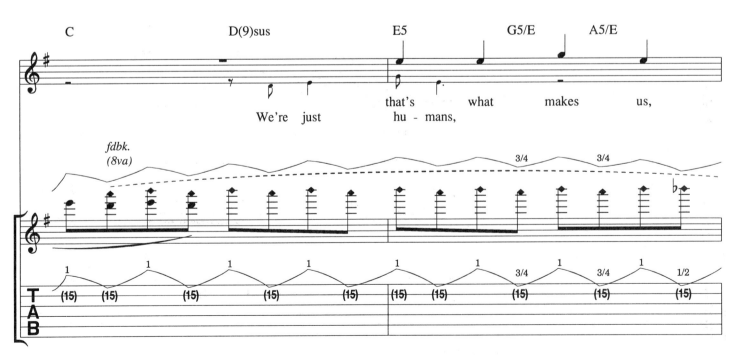

Humans Being – 13 – 11
PG9665

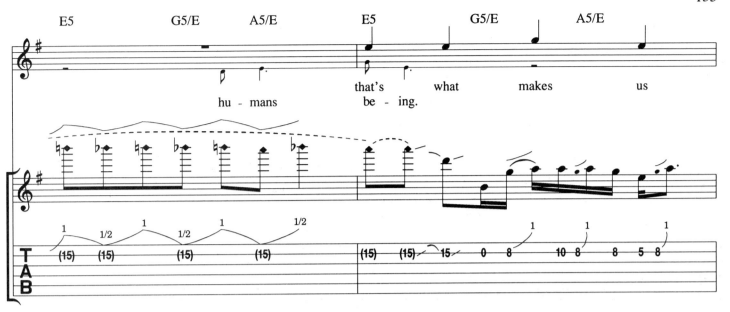

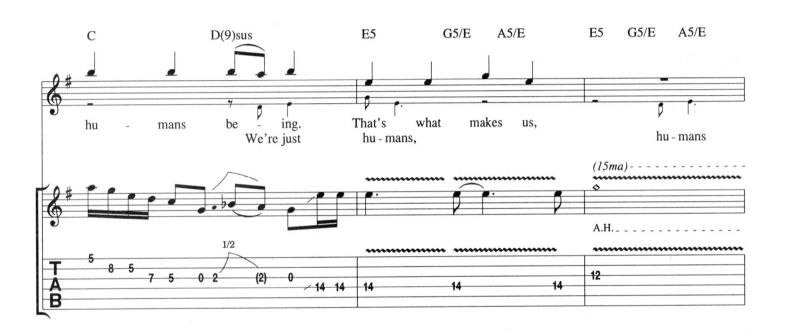

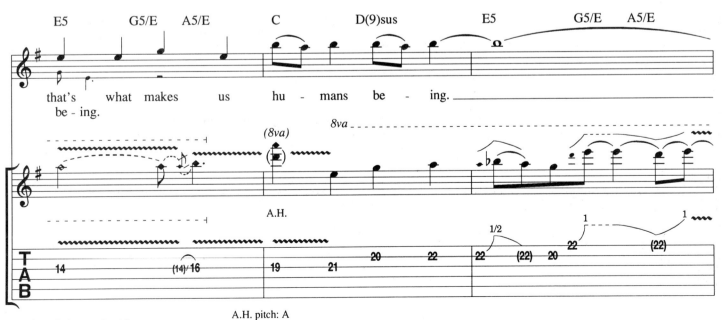

A.H. pitch: A

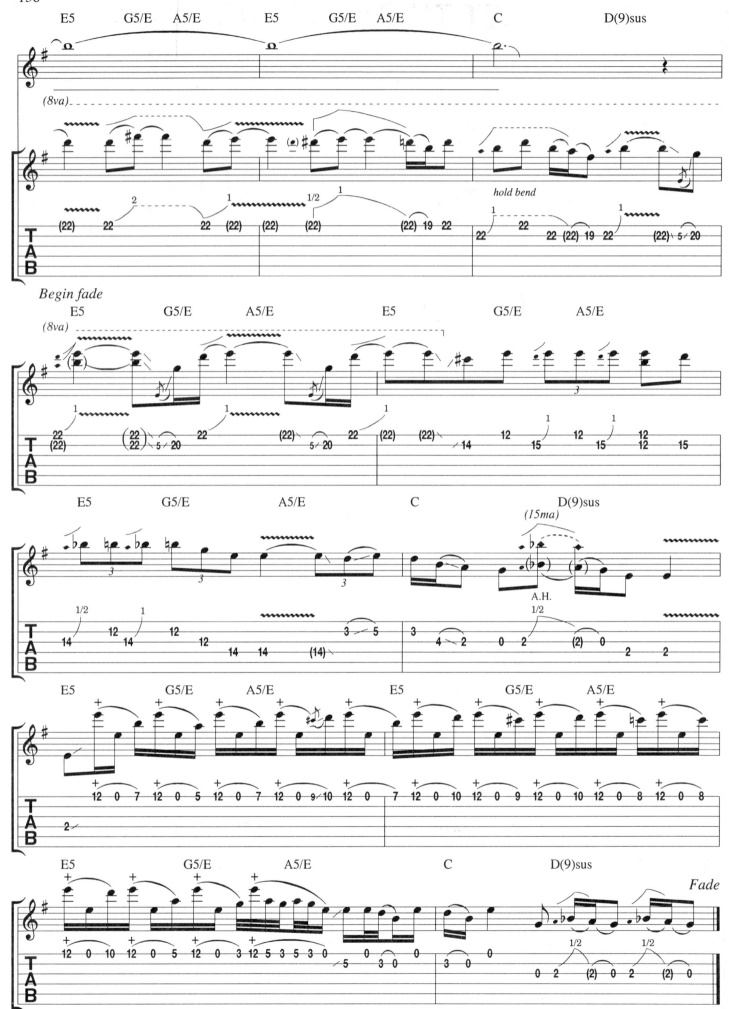

Humans Being – 13 – 13
PG9665

CAN'T GET THIS STUFF NO MORE

Words and Music by
EDDIE VAN HALEN, ALEX VAN HALEN,
MICHAEL ANTHONY and DAVID LEE ROTH

All gtrs. use Drop D tuning:
⑥ = D

Moderate rock shuffle ♩. = 100
Intro:

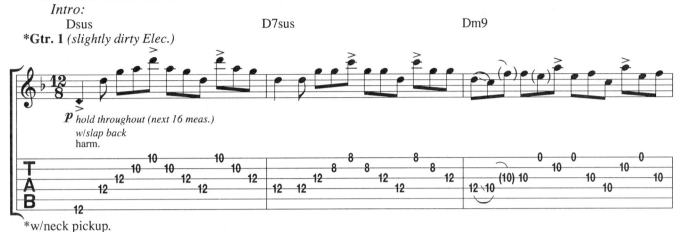

*w/neck pickup.

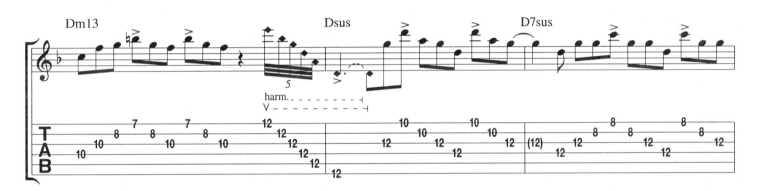

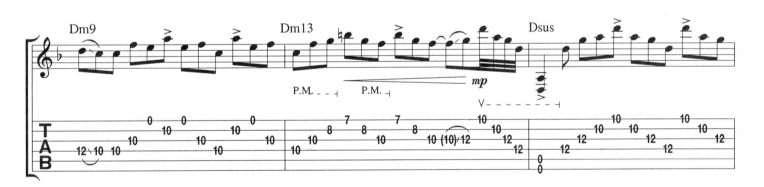

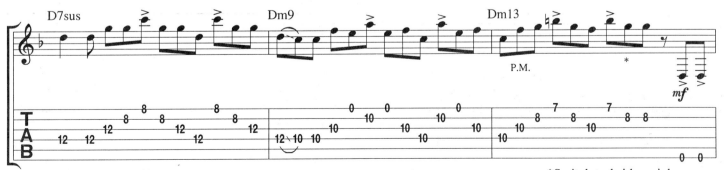

*Switch to bridge pickup.

Can't Get This Stuff No More – 16 – 1
PG9665

138

I don't need __ so much to re - mem - ber, __ no, no. __

w/Rhy. Fill 1 *(Gtr. 1) 1st time*
w/Rhy. Fill 2 *(Gtr. 1) 2nd time*

___ That's __ how it is _____ when you tell ___ the truth. ___ *Oh!*

* % Chorus 1, 2 & 3:

1.3. How man - y times __ does some - bod - y lie _____ 'til
2. *See additional lyrics*

Gtr. 1

Gtr. 2 (dist.)

*w/vocal ad lib. on D.S.
**Depress bar before striking note (next 3 meas.)

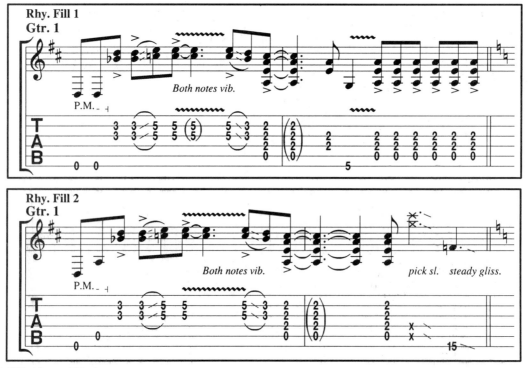

Rhy. Fill 1
Gtr. 1

Both notes vib.

Rhy. Fill 2
Gtr. 1

Both notes vib. *pick sl. steady gliss.*

142

Can't Get This Stuff No More – 16 – 7
PG9665

144

*Gtr. 1 doubled simile by organ at this point (next 8 meas.)

Can't Get This Stuff No More – 16 – 8
PG9665

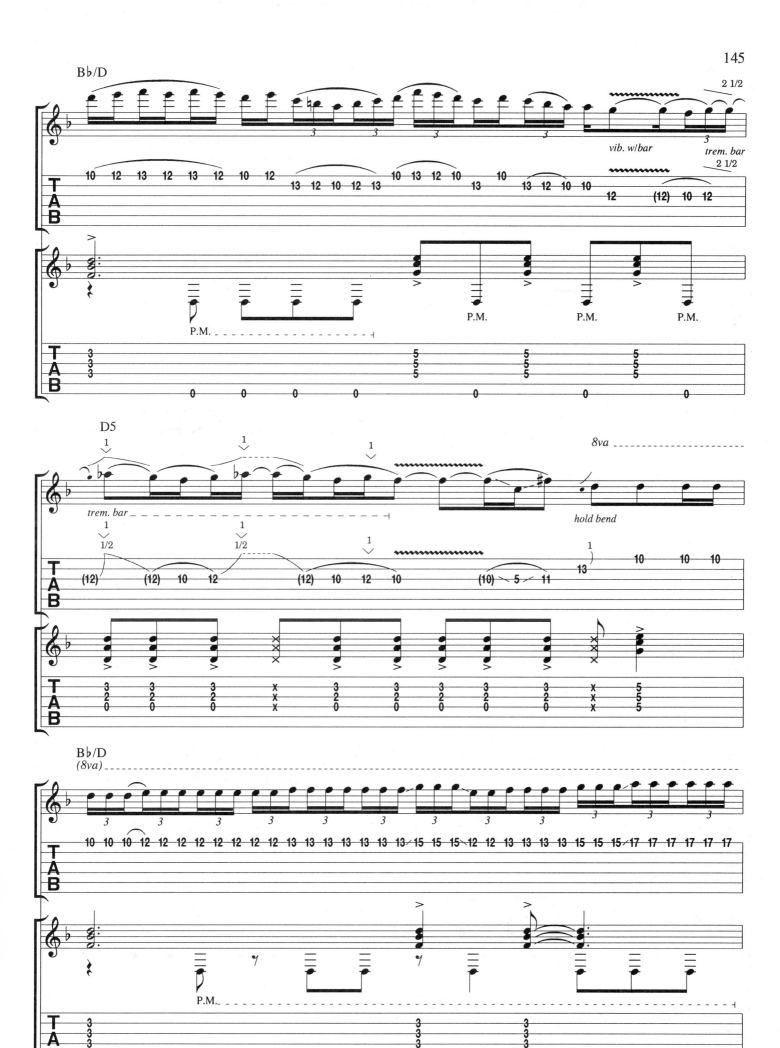

Can't Get This Stuff No More – 16 – 9
PG9665

146

Can't Get This Stuff No More – 16 – 10
PG9665

*Depress bar before striking note (next 5 meas.)

Can't Get This Stuff No More – 16 – 11
PG9665

148

150

Can't Get This Stuff No More – 16 – 15
PG9665

Verse 2:
That's the thing 'bout self-improvement.
Don't get me wrong, I plan to get some soon.
Outside the wire something's moving.
My barn burnt down, now I can see the moon.
(To Chorus 2:)

Chorus 2:
A slice at a time, like a pizza pie.
You serve up the truth, I don't want it anymore.
Keep that in mind when we say goodbye,
'Cause you can't get this stuff no more.

ME WISE MAGIC

Words and Music by
**EDDIE VAN HALEN, ALEX VAN HALEN,
MICHAEL ANTHONY and DAVID LEE ROTH**

All guitar parts were recorded using a Steinberger guitar equipped with a patented "Trans Trem." tremolo system. The "Trans Trem." is a locking tremolo bar that functions as a "quick-capo" by evenly raising or lowering the pitches of all of the strings and then locking the bridge into the new key.

This arrangement was written for standard guitars. For example, the first eight measures were recorded with the "Trans Trem." locked a whole tone sharp. To emulate this technique, place a capo at the the 2nd fret and remove it during the 8th measure. When using the capo, treat the 2nd fret in the tablature as open. Repeat this procedure when indicated.

154

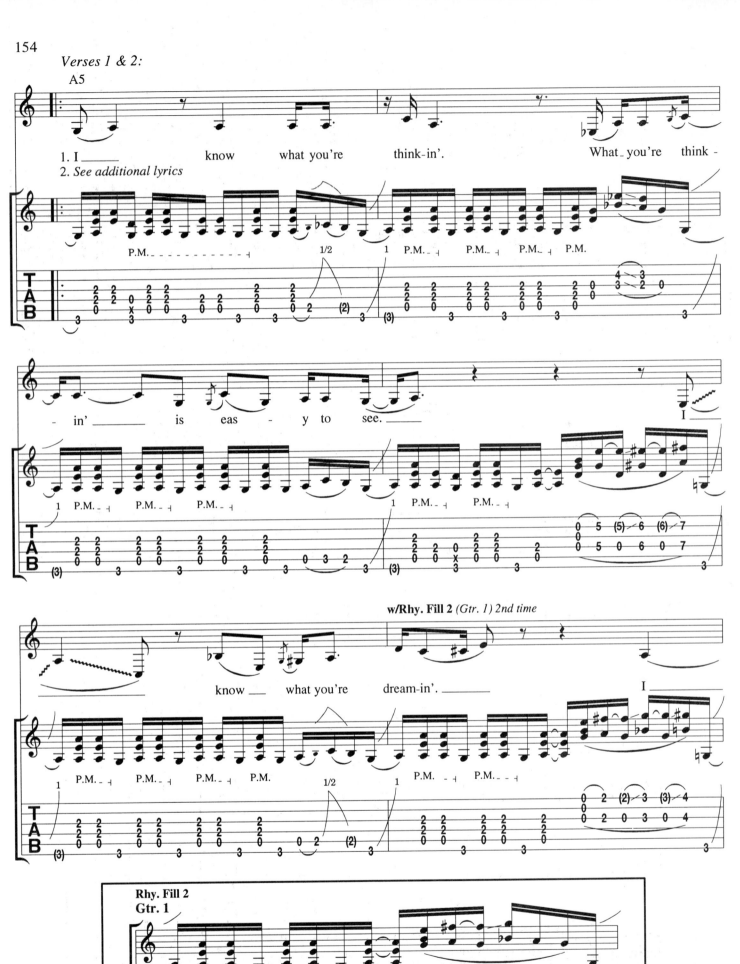

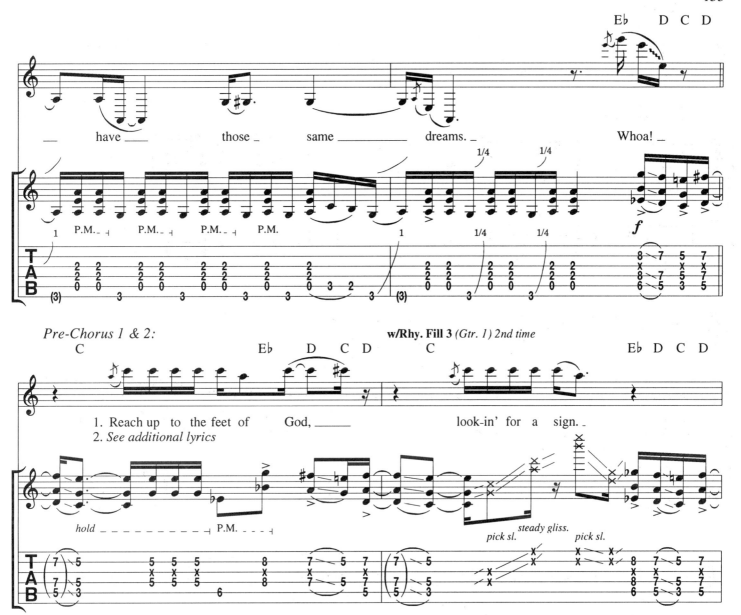

have ___ those _ same _____ dreams. _ Whoa! _

Pre-Chorus 1 & 2:

w/Rhy. Fill 3 *(Gtr. 1) 2nd time*

1. Reach up to the feet of God, _____ look-in' for a sign.
2. *See additional lyrics*

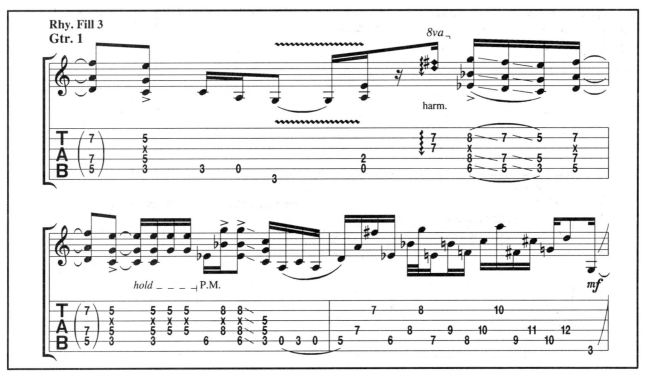

Rhy. Fill 3
Gtr. 1

Chorus:
w/Fill 1 *(Gtr. 3) 2nd time*
w/Fill 3 *(Gtr. 3) 3rd time*

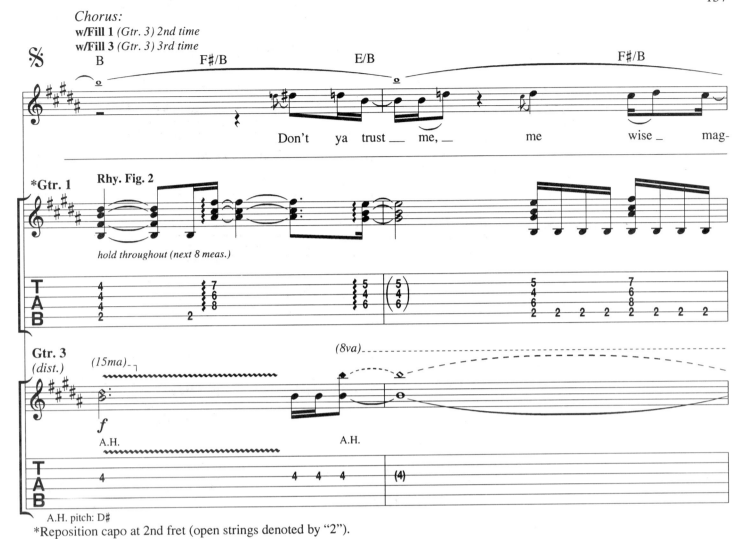

Don't ya trust __ me, __ me wise __ mag-

*Reposition capo at 2nd fret (open strings denoted by "2").

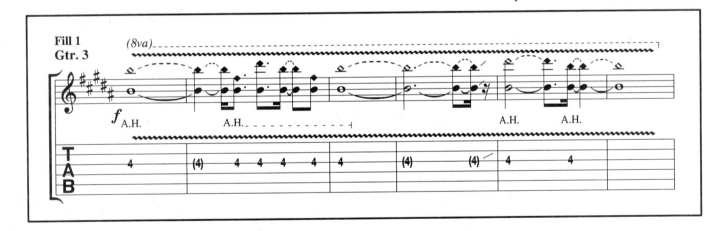

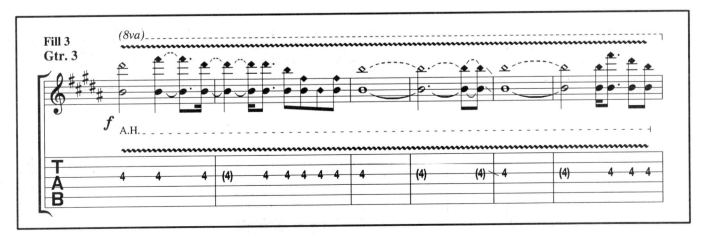

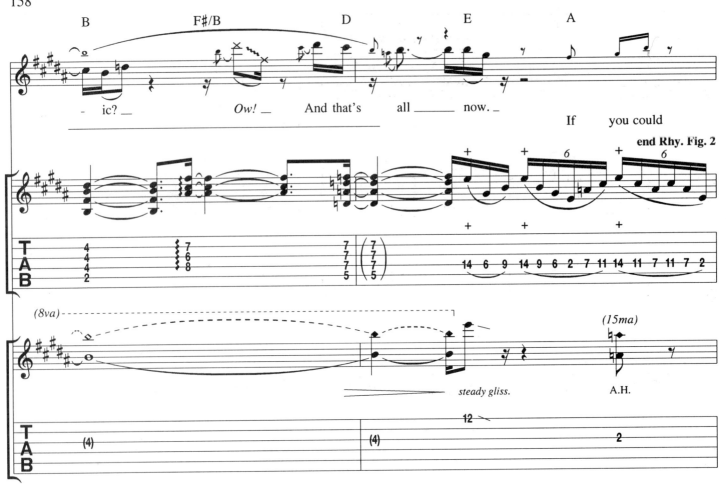

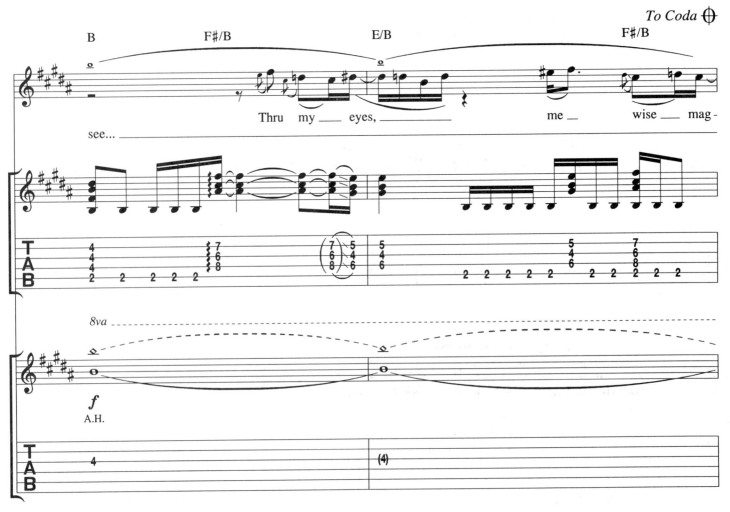

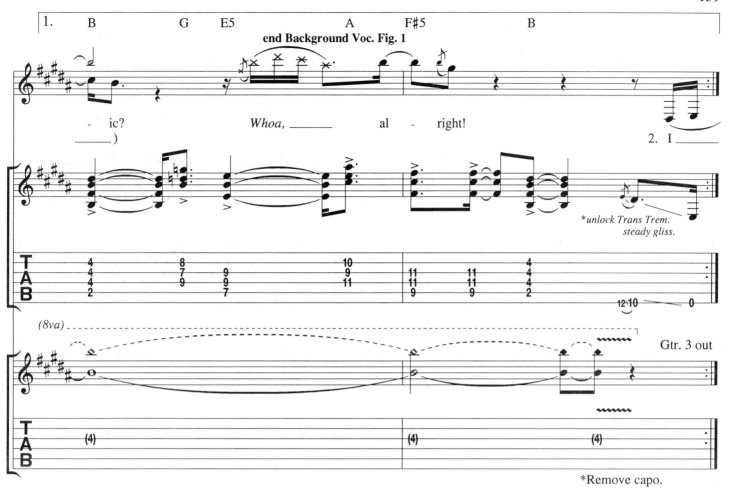

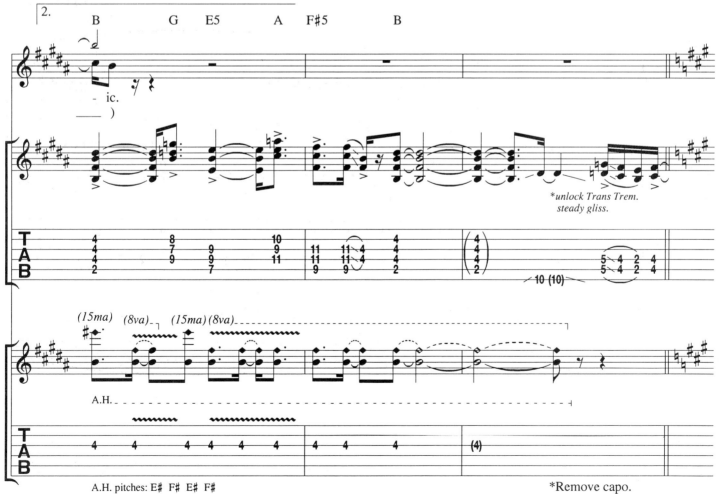

Interlude:

*Tonality implied by bass gtr.

Guitar Solo:

*Depress bar before striking note.

166